PIANO • VOCAL • GUITAR

VH1 20 GREAT POWER BALLADS

ISBN 978-1-4234-5817-3

HAL•LEONARD®
CORPORATION
7777 W. BLUEMOUND RD. P.O. BOX 13819 MILWAUKEE, WI 53213

Visit Hal Leonard Online at
www.halleonard.com

AGAIN

Words and Music by
LENNY KRAVITZ

BETH

Words and Music by BOB EZRIN,
STANLEY PENRIDGE and PETER CRISS

Rock Ballad, with feeling

Beth, I hear _ you call - in', but I can't come home right now. _
You say you feel _ so emp - ty, that our house just ain't a home. _

Me and the boys _ are play - in' and we just can't find the sound. _
I'm al - ways some - where else _ and _ you're al - ways there a - lone. _

CLOSE MY EYES FOREVER

Words and Music by LITA FORD
and OZZY OSBOURNE

Moderately, in 2

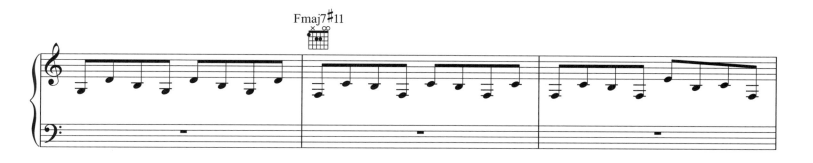

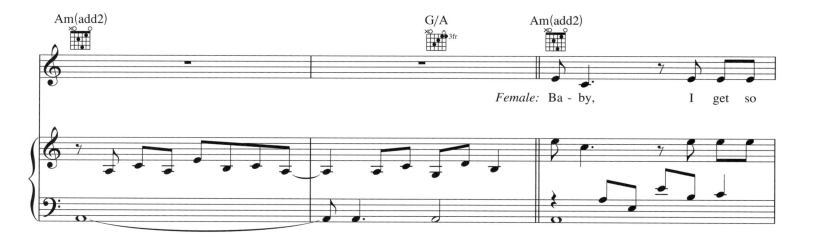

Female: Ba - by, I get so

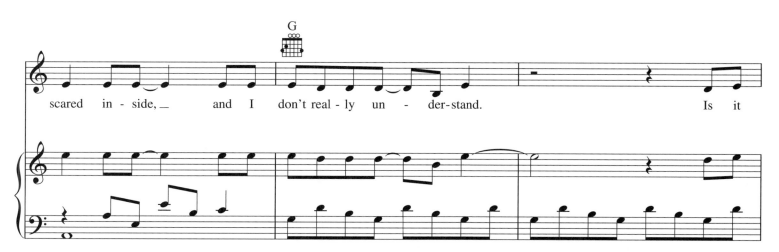

scared in - side, __ and I don't real - ly un - der - stand. Is it

Male and female vocals are all written in their sounding octave.

ev - er,   will it

all re - main ___ the same? _____

To Coda ⊕

Will you

ev - er take ___ me?   *Male:* No,   I   just   can't   take   the   pain. ___

Female: Would you ev - er trust ___ me?

Male: No, I'll nev - er feel ___ the same. ___

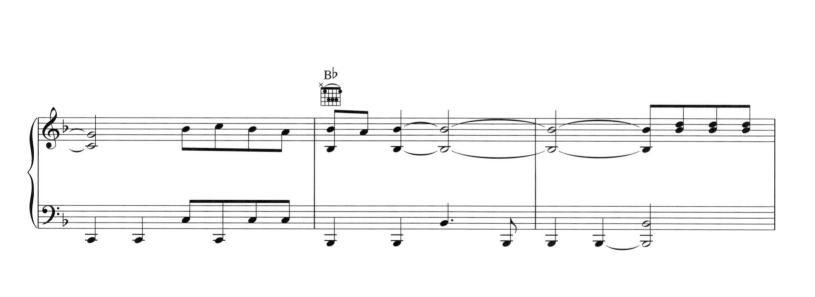

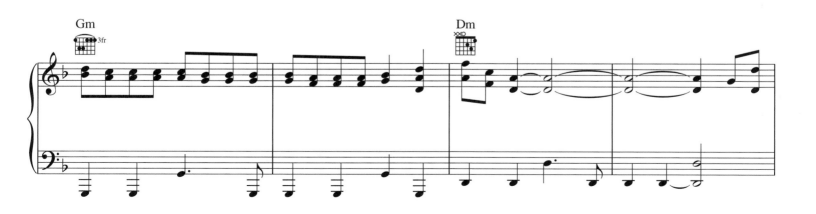

DON'T KNOW WHAT YOU GOT
(Till It's Gone)

Words and Music by
TOM KEIFER

23

HOME SWEET HOME

Words and Music by TOMMY LEE
and NIKKI SIXX

EVERY ROSE HAS ITS THORN

Words and Music by BOBBY DALL,
BRETT MICHAELS, BRUCE JOHANNESSON and RIKKI ROCKETT

I REMEMBER YOU

Words and Music by RACHEL BOLAN
and DAVE "THE SNAKE" SABO

Woke up to the sound __ of pour-ing __ rain. __

The wind would whis-per __ and I'd think of __ you, __

and all the tears __ you cried __ that called my __ name. __

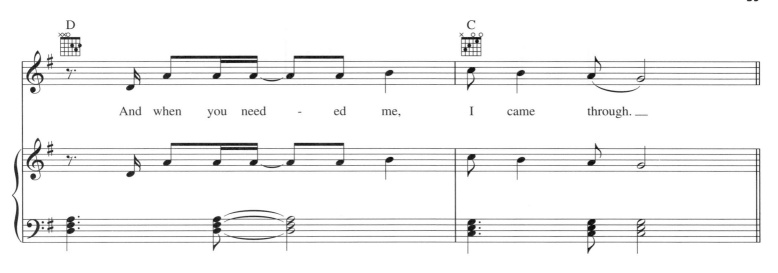

And when you need - ed me, I came through. ___

I paint a pic - ture of the days gone __ by, ___
We spent the sum - mer with the top rolled down. ___
Woke up to __ the sound of pour - ing __ rain. ___

when love went blind and you would make me __ see. ___
Wished ev - er af - ter would be like __ this. ___
Washed a - way a dream of __ you. ___

I'd stare a life - time in - to your ___ eyes _____
You said "I love you, babe" with - out a _____ sound. _____
But noth - ing else could ev - er take you a - way. _____

so that I knew ___ that you were there for ___ me. _____
I said I'd give ___ my life for just one ___ kiss. _____
'Cause you'll al - ways be my dream come ___ true. _____

Time af - ter time ___ you were ___ there for _____ me. _____
I'd live for your smile, _ and ___ die for your kiss. _____
Oh, my dar - lin', I love ___ you. _____

prom - ise that we made._____ Well, I swear you'll nev - er be lone - ly.____

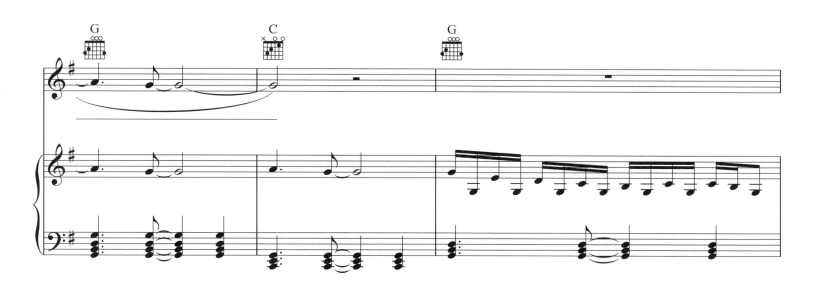

I re - mem - ber, I re - mem - ber_____

I'LL BE THERE FOR YOU

Words and Music by JON BON JOVI
and RICHIE SAMBORA

IS THIS LOVE

Words and Music by DAVID COVERDALE
and JOHN SYKES

IT'S BEEN AWHILE

Words and Music by AARON LEWIS, MICHAEL MUSHOK,
JONATHAN WYSOCKI and JOHN APRIL

And it's a-while
And it's a-while
And it's a-while

since I____ could
since I____ could say
since I____ could

hold____ my head____ up high.____
that I was-n't ad-dic-ted.____
look____ at my-self straight.____

* Recorded a half step lower

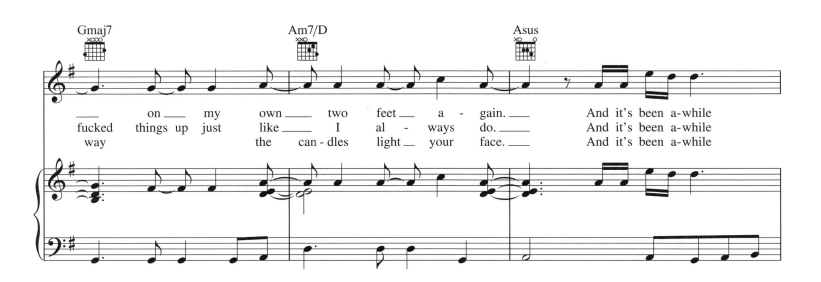

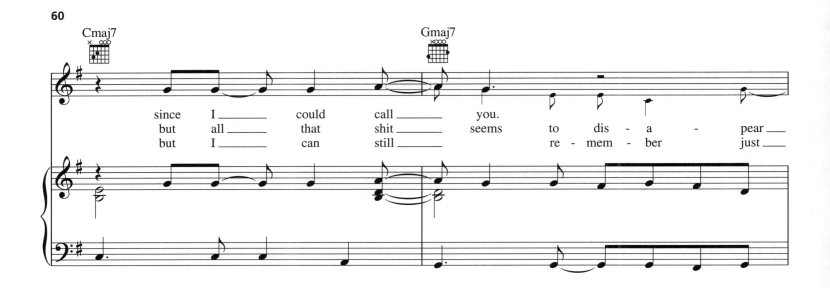

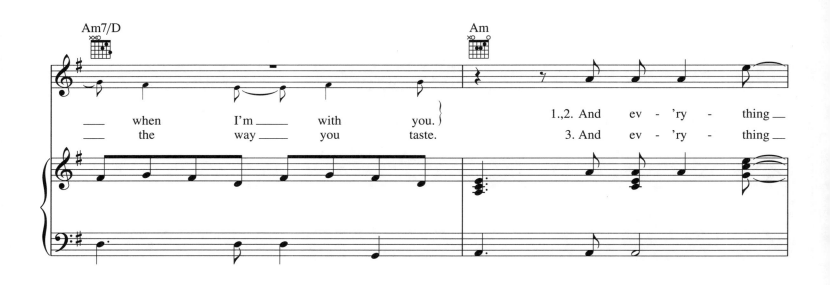

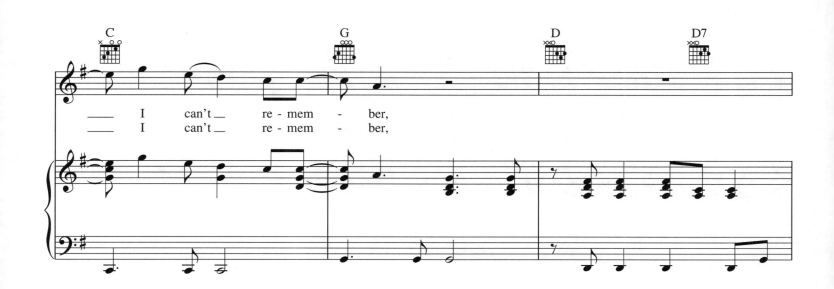

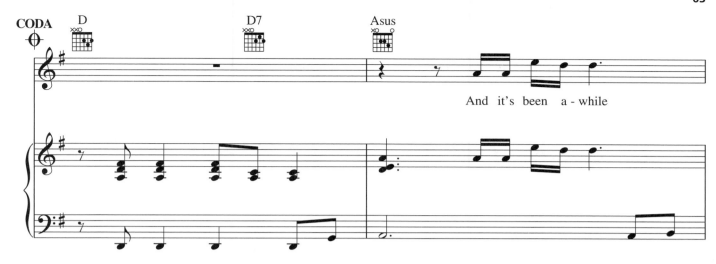

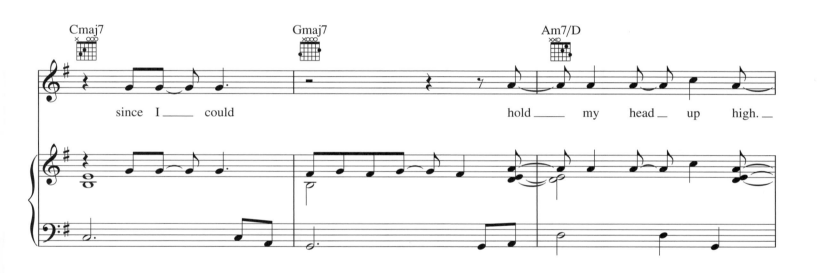

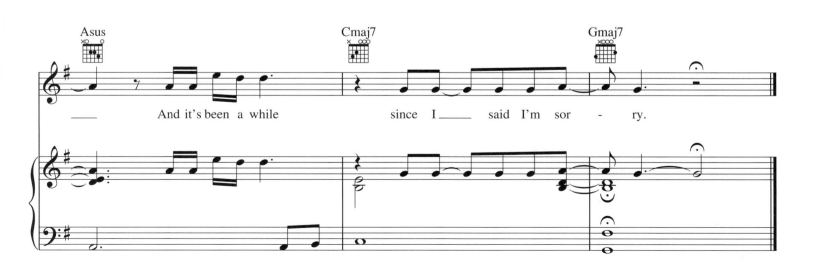

KEEP ON LOVING YOU

Words and Music by
KEVIN CRONIN

You should have seen by the look in my eyes,_ ba - by, there was some - thin' miss - in'._

_ You should have known by the tone of my voice,_ may - be,

but you did - n't lis - ten. __ You played dead,

but you nev-er bled. In-stead you laid still in the grass __ all coiled up and hiss-

- in'. __ And though I know all a-

Instrumental

bout those men, __ still I don't re-mem-ber. __

'Cause it was us, ba-by, way be-fore them, __ and we're still to-geth-er. __

LOVE BITES

Words and Music by JOE ELLIOTT,
PHIL COLLEN, RICHARD SAVAGE, RICHARD ALLEN,
STEVE CLARK and ROBERT JOHN "MUTT" LANGE

2nd time Guitar solo

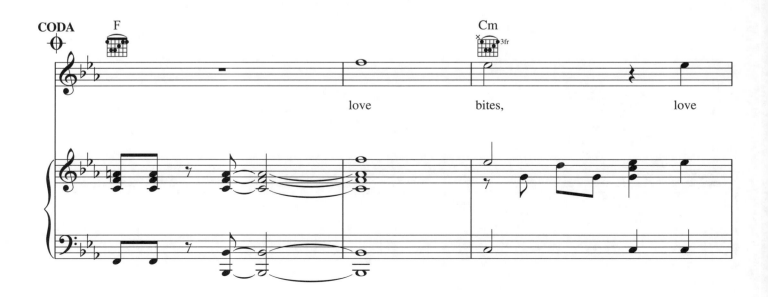

love   bites,   love

LOVE SONG

Words and Music by JEFFREY KEITH
and FRANK HANNON

Keep an o - pen heart and you'll find love a - gain, __ I know. you'll find love a - gain, __ I

know.

(Instrumental solo)

OPEN ARMS

Words and Music by STEVE PERRY
and JONATHAN CAIN

NOVEMBER RAIN

Words and Music by
W. AXL ROSE

Recorded a half step lower.

Some-times I need some time on my own. _____ Some-times I

need some time all a - lone. _____ Ooh, _____ ev-'ry-bod-y needs some time on their own. _

_____ Ooh, _____ don't you know you need some time all a - lone? _____

And when your fears_ sub - side __

_____ and shad - ows still __ re - main, _____

SILENT LUCIDITY

Words and Music by
CHRIS DeGARMO

*1st time vocal is sung one octave lower than written.

am smil - ing next to you _____ in

si - lent lu - cid - i - ty. _____

(Spoken:) Visualize your dreams.   Record it in the present tense.   Put it into a permanent form.

If you persist in your efforts,   you can achieve dream control...

D.S. al Coda
(take 2nd ending)

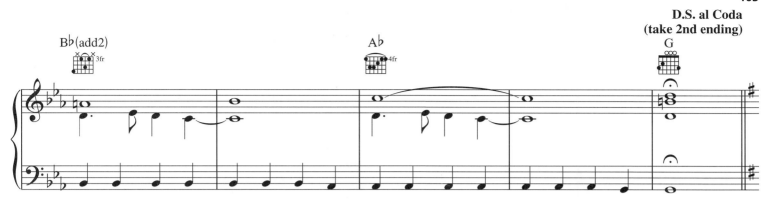

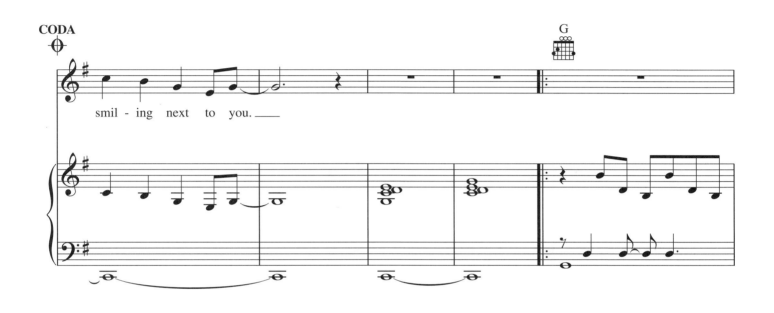

smil - ing next to you. _____

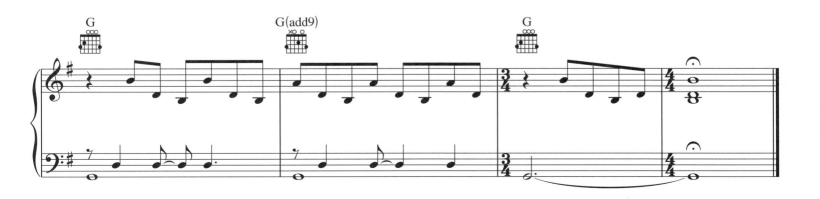

STILL LOVING YOU

Words and Music by KLAUS MEINE
and RUDOLF SCHENKER

THESE DREAMS

Words and Music by MARTIN GEORGE PAGE
and BERNIE TAUPIN

Spare a lit-tle can-dle, save some light for me;
Is it cloak and dag-ger? Could it be spring or fall?
The sweet-est song is si-lence that I've ev-er heard.

fig-ures up a-head mov-ing in the trees. White
I walk with-out a cut through a stained-glass wall.
Fun-ny how your feet in dreams nev-er touch the earth. In a

WITH ARMS WIDE OPEN

Words and Music by MARK TREMONTI
and SCOTT STAPP

121

SISTER CHRISTIAN

Words and Music by
KELLY KEAGY

Moderate Rock

Sis - ter Chris - tian, oh, the
Babe, you know you're grow - ing

time has come, ___
up so fast ___

and you know that you're ___ the on - ly one ___ to say ___
and mom-ma's wor - ry - ing ___ that you won't last to say ___

O. K. ___
let's play. ___

Where you go - ing what ___ you
Sis - ter Chris - tian, there's ___ so